Are You Proud of Me?

Poems by
Alex Dang!

Cover and Interior art by Lora Mathis
Editor: Clementine von Radics

Published in Portland, Oregon, by Where Are You Press

For all the nights that said
there would be no morning for me

Table of Contents

"I used to care what people thought,
but now I care more."

-Childish Gambino

3 a.m. in Portland

i imagine writing
about you is to

go back and unwrap bandages
only to gag douse the hurt

in gasoline and flirt
with the bonfire

that has been devouring
our pictures

Another Choice

Let's call it as it is:
I am afraid to be honest,
too shit scared to walk uncharted.

When I was five,
I wasn't afraid of the dark.
It wasn't because I was brave;
I just didn't know there was another option.
I hadn't been taught fear yet.

If all you know is courage,
if all you know is truth,
it's so easy to be a lion.

When I learned
vulnerability
versus
toughness,

it made sense to be the hammer.
But the nails hold the house together.

I Never Wanted to Write This Poem

I am 17 when he brandishes a knife
and a tongue that he kisses someone
he loves with. He tells me to
Empty Your Wallet Ching Chong
And You Won't Get Hurt
and I raise my hands to smack down
like a mousetrap against his throat
only to run like hell into Walmart
and I wait there for a few minutes
before continuing my walk back home.

I don't tell my mom.
I sit down and have dinner with my dad.

I am 18 when he shows me a gun
with hands that are too shaky
to hold anything, the barrel swaying
and his swastika tattoo a blur,
so I empty my pockets and he dips
into the night like a man driving home
on Christmas Eve.

I don't tell my dad.
I sit down and have dinner with my mom.

I am 19 when I am pulled over
and the officer speaks slowly to me,
his words clumsy syrup making its
cloying, awkward way down my ears
and I tell him that I was late for
meeting a date. His eyes widen
like a full plate, grateful that the
kid sitting in the car in front of him
can speak all American, like
his favorite holiday special.
He drives off and

I don't tell my date.
I sit down and have dinner with her.

I am 20 when I am jumped by
five masked college boys. Indifference,
ignorance, drunkenness, it's hard to say
but I assign them meaning. Senseless
violence scares me too much.
I chalk it up to prejudice, Halloween,
an invincibility that goes with being
anonymous, a hooded villain, a jackass
with four other equally jackass friends.

What gives me away?
Most days I think myself
an easy target. I'm small and wiry,
looking like any push could
break me. Like I was born from
honey and I'm a toffee-skinned boy
too naïve, too sunshine to know better.
I've known worse.

I wasn't born with a swivel neck
or with knuckles that have touched
another person's blood. I was
forced to learn,
forced to fight,
forced to run.

And I don't blame them for any of it.
I stare at the mirror
resisting the urge to break it.
And they goad me to do it.
It's the one thing we can agree on:

we don't like the way he looks.

Too Little Too Much

Some days
I am the bull.

Some nights
I am the china shop.

Far too often
I am both.

The Elephant Garden

Eddie Huang loves Hip-Hop.

Eddie tucks himself into a
too-big armor of sagging jeans,
wide shirt, fitted cap,
and dresses his tongue with slang
found between the fangs
of Hip-Hop tracks.

As he does this,
Eddie buffs up:

adds a foot to his penis,
calls him and his boys Big Dick Asians,
becomes a real man.

Wants to push the envelope
like real men do,
so pushes down women
like real men do.
Listens to Jeezy's Thug Motivation
and would kill him
to wear that snowman chain.

Hides behind this
thick bravado,
thick like elephant skin.
He wants it to be known
that his thickness is an elephant
and the elephant in the room.

My masculinity is
rooted in the rumor
of my penis being little
and this belittlement
has caused everything to be
about my anatomy.

Once, someone joked that
I needed a microscope to jerk off.
The girl I had a crush on in middle school

asked me if it was true that all Asian guys are small.
Someone shouted at me at a bus stop,
Fuck A Chinese Dude And Still Be Horny 30 Minutes Later!

It's so common for us Asian Boys
to find our manhood in Hip-Hop—
this culture of I'm The Best
And I Will Tell You Why.

We feel taller in these
Timberland boots.
Our speech becomes
slow, loud, and bumping:
each sentence a stone slab,
more proof of our hardness.

When the world
deems us
weak and small,
calls us sick men of Asia,
puts us on one side of the scale and
scales us down to a punchline,
we show up with
the definition of fight
wrapped between our fists.

We reclaim our masculinity
after years of clear-cutting.
But instead of replanting our forest,
we want to swing the axes
like real men do.

We show off, freshly bruised and bloody
as we are doted on by a gaggle of models.
Show America that this is what an Asian Man is
as we grip wood grain in one hand
and her ponytail in the other.

We are so vicious in our fight
to not be what you think we are
that we become what you think we are:

scared boys pushing our insecurities

into the mud because that's how you
show someone you like them,

right?

Letters to My Father
by Ash Ketchum

Dear Dad,
I left home today to become the very best.
Is that why you're still out there?

Dear Dad,
My Metapod evolved!
He started off so small but today
he sprouted rainbows from his back
and protected me from danger.
One day I'll show you how strong I've gotten.

Dear Dad,
Mom doesn't tell me about you,
but I think it's cuz you're
so cool and great and awesome
that she doesn't want me to get jealous.
I don't get why she hides
your photos though.

Dear Dad,
I haven't been home in months
and I'm starting to miss it.
How do you stay away for so long?

Dear Dad,
I just left Lavender Town and
everything was soaked in
death and ghosts and purple.
Is that your favorite color?
I think I saw you.

Dear Dad,
There's this girl I like.
But I'm not sure if I like-like her.
How did you know you liked Mom?

Dear Dad,
I lost to someone so strong but
today I came back and won!
I didn't run away! So why did you?

Dear Dad,
Mom called and asked
When Are You Coming Home
I told her I Don't Know.

Did you have the same conversation?

Dear Dad,
My friends said that I cry in my sleep,
which is silly; I don't have sad dreams.
I usually dream about Mom and me
and you.

Dear Dad,
We were playing a game where we
matched moves to our personalities.
Misty is surf because she takes us
places no one else could.
Brock is strength because he never
lets obstacles stand in our way.
They said I was flash because
I'm the light at the end of the tunnel.

What would you be?
Probably *fly*.
Or cut.

Dear Dad,
I came home today and remembered
why I wanted to leave.

Dear Dad,
I came home today and never
wanted to leave.

Dear Dad,
I love you.

Dear Dad,
I don't care if you're not the very best.
You should come home.

Dear Dad,
Every day I try harder and harder and harder
to answer all these questions that you left

behind.

The Swallowed

Francisco Goya paints
Saturn Devouring His Son,
depicting the Titan king
in gory frenzy, consuming
one of his six children.

The myth tells us that Saturn
heard a prophecy that one of his children
would usurp him, like Saturn with
his father. Fear fills his stomach
and the only remedy is
the flesh of his flesh.

Ilya Repin paints
Ivan the Terrible and His Son Ivan on Friday, 16 November 1581,
showing Ivan the Terrible
clutching his child
on trampled carpet
seconds after
bludgeoning him.

The history tells us that Ivan the Terrible
saw rebellion in his son's eyes and
terrible hands became stronger than he,
possessed with holding on to power
by beating it out of his child.

The poet paints
himself bloodied and wild
as he empties his heart.

The story tells us that a boy
whose chest was heavier
than his frame cracked
it open, desperate to
hollow the fullness.

In these three paintings,
you see anguish.

Their eyes
are the same:

They are so scared
of what they are doing
to themselves.

Harbor

I try writing a poem about masculinity. I take out the punch-shaped anchor box: ready to torpedo the sucker open and my mom calls.

So I pick up and we talk. And talk. And talk. The calling is new for me. I mean, back when I lived under her roof we never spoke. High school was rough on both of us. See, I always put my then girlfriend before my mom's feelings. The big argument we had sounded like rushing water filling up the cabin of a sinking ship and it ended quiet: our home now sunken boat. Things change though. I'm 21 now, and my mom chats me up about anything. Everything.

I'm looking at this poem the entire time we're talking, as open as a palm asking me to hold it.

She's finishing up after like 45 minutes and she says Dad Wants To Talk To You and I say Okay and me and my dad have the same talk we have every time. My dad says Hey and I say Hey Dad and he tells me to Make Sure There's Water In Your Car's Radiator and I say Okay and I ask him How Is Work is and he says Smooth Sailing and I say That's Good and then we let a small silence be born, swim upstream, and die before we say good-bye. We rarely talk past treading.

I look back at the poem, this clenched ball of wrought iron and chewed fingernails, and decide to put it back inside me.

I put the hand back in my chest and it starts the squall and the thrash, throws my heart a haymaker, and continues to chaos. I don't let anyone see it. Only I feel the swell and bruise like a high tide behind my skin, but anyone who gets close enough to me can hear this barrage rattling my torso like a boat in a bottle in a storm in this bottle so the hand corks my throat so you can't hear the hollow seashell body beg imperfect storm. It climbs up and shuts my mouth and I bury this poem again.

What We Don't Say

There's a lot of shit we don't talk about in my family.

I have never had the sex talk.
We don't talk politics, or racism,
or sexism, or any kind of ism for that matter.

We are a polite family.
We are very good at not talking about, like,
real things.

So when once I mentioned to my mom
that I wanted to kill myself and I wasn't sure if it was
normal to feel that way and she said

> I've Wanted to Kill Myself Too.
> You Don't Think I've Wanted to Give Up?

we just never talked about it again,
only looked away from each other
politely.

There's a gorgeous struggle in
living in a house fire; the rising
temperature as a reminder that Hell
is always trying to capture you,
but failing.

There's a degree of beauty
in telling yourself that everything is alright.
The same beauty that allows us to drown a casket
in flowers.

Lately, we are becoming
more stubborn than persistent.

We are too prideful, my family.
God, how we boast how easily blood
washes off our skin. How we hold
so much value in our ability to bury.
Us, a band of gravediggers, never
climbing out, only hollowing enough dirt

to get us through to the other end.

My dad has had so much taken from him.
Learned how hard it is to put flesh back on the bone.
Realized it's simpler to let dead things stay dead.

But we are so much a people of resurrection.
We have been reborn in this country out
of the cremation ashes. Forged our bodies
from sacrifice and have known too well
how to speak with the dying because
we are always talking to ourselves.

I think that's it.
Why my family
doesn't speak
mental illness.

Decided to hide
PTSD from a war or
entering a country that only
speaks slur to your wife and children
away in the attic.
Why we refuse to address
this burning home:

Because we are so magic.
What we say we become.
We say we are fine.
We say we are Dangs.
We say our name like the blessing it is.

All we have to our name is our name
and we will gladly die for it.

And I am scared we will.

in which the poet tries to apologize again

i am sorry i tried calling you that one time
when i was drunk off lonely and whiskey and four loko

its just that your hands were so good at keeping
me together my body still sometimes collapses into the shape

of your mouth i am a soft malleable thing and it has taken me
too long to realize that you are also this more important

that you are more than my memories that you exist free
and independent of my life that my idea of you that crosses

my empty highway mind is not you and with this i am so sorry
for all the nights i tried to split your heart open just so

i had a place to rest i did not understand how you were no
longer me anymore how the you i had in me was a postcard

and not the city forgive the fury the angry prayers tossed at
the dark of my 3 a.m. ceiling that were meant for your neck

you were asleep the night when we were breaking and my
skin felt taut and wanting to scream but cassidy

told me that it makes sense why this was so frustrating
the rusting of four years should make me mad it meant i cared

i still get the urge to hollow my arms so you can fit better you
this new person who has grown and loved and spilled over into

a newer night i forget so often i cant carry you like i did
and that you dont know how to hold me like before

im still apologizing

"Dreaming up a day that I could say
the world is ours"

-Childish Gambino

4 p.m. in Boston

youre living different you dont stay up
as late as you used to and you think of her
even less now you have new goals and
new shoes in fact you have been shedding
so much light on tomorrow that it throws
major league shade on yesterday
it helps it helps that youre getting out
it helps that you dont cringe from old
bookmarks anymore—youre letting things rest
sleep easy i know youve gnawed the bones
of nostalgia but the marrow is dried and white
its time to cremate the past and
blow the ashes unceremoniously behind

youve spent so much of today
as a shrine to last night

Seriously, What Kind of Asian Are You?

So he said to me...

What Kind of Asian Are You?
100% Chow Chow.

Don't All Asian Guys Have Small Dicks?
They still work.
There are literally billions of us.
How do you think we got here otherwise?

All Asian People Look Alike.
You must have been the shittiest Guess Who? player.

How Do You See out of Your Eyes?
Because everything is in widescreen!

Because I make the jokes faster
and better than you.
Because anything you've said
I've spun into my arsenal.

Because what's scarier
than the monster's
bloodstained sheets,
face ancient and decaying,
teeth glinting gravedigger shovels,
what's more terrifying than
nightmare sinew,
carnage on tongue,
hands craving necks,
what's more powerful?

Looking him in the eyes,
laughing because he does not get it,
pinching his cheeks like the scared child he is,
and washing the dried, caked-on past off his sheets
and bleaching it white, clean, clean, white.

Hang it up. It's waving.
This symbol of whiteness,
now surrender.

I Will Always Love H.E.R.

Kendrick Lamar
splits open monsters
and fights on the virtue
that to get stronger,
you go to battle only with armies
that are capable of stampede.
Those who tread lightly
are not worthy
of your warpath.

Lupe Fiasco
ties his tongue
into a cat's cradle.
Whispers sweet everythings
into the ears of middle-schoolers
who by the end of the song
will know the brutality
of the Audubon Ballroom.

Talib Kweli
lectures behind a podium
with Howard Zinn
to college-somethings
about the nature of history:
Everyone is a writer
but not the best authors pen the past.
Only the victorious do.

A columnist in the New York Daily News said that Hip-Hop emphasizes The Crudest
Materialism in Which the Ultimate Goal Is Money and It Did Not Matter How One
Got It.

Jay-Z
sits on the steps of his former
housing project with Oprah Winfrey,
then shakes the hand
of the most powerful man
in the free world.
He and Beyoncé
are American royalty,
and their bloodlines

are unconcerned with their
humble origins.

50 Cent
demonstrates a contrasting irony
as he watches his money
grow up to be worth his namesake
a million fold,
and then some.

Sean Combs
drapes the resting place
of The Notorious B.I.G. in jewels
as he whispers to his best friend,
Don't Worry, I Made Us Enough Money
That It'll Follow Me into the Afterlife.
We'll Be More Than Taken Care of
When We Meet Again.

Republican senator Chris McDaniel was quoted as saying that Hip-Hop Is A Culture
That Values Rap And The Destruction Of Community Values More Than It Does
Poetry.

Kanye West and Nina Simone
swing-dance in an orchard
as the farmers all around them
peddle their strange fruit.

Tupac Shakur
figures out the equation
for immortality: It is
6 albums,
8 movies,
and an understanding that
power moves create fame,
influential motion crafts legacy.

André 3000
writes a song about the
devastating separation
between himself and his love.
The world cannot help

but pulse to it.

Andre, knowing this,
before the second chorus
in "Hey Ya!," laments:
Y'all Don't Wanna Hear Me.
You Just Wanna Dance.

Across the internet, Hip-Hop is not regarded as a musical genre. Criticized for lack
of originality, vapid lyrics, and a monotonous sound, the overwhelming statement
is that Hip-Hop has nothing to do with music.

RZA and Just Blaze
sit behind monitors and soundboards
as they summon the spirits of
Bill Withers,
Gladys Knight,
and Curtis Mayfield
into the studio.

Hip-Hop has nothing to do with music.

Nicki Minaj
simpers and then
spits ferocious
in the face of kings
as they watch the queen conquer.
Female-named hurricanes kill more
than do their male counterparts.

Hip-Hop has nothing to do with music.

This beat
slam rumbles through your
'98 Toyota Camry speakers
and transforms these
3 minutes and 32 seconds
into a parade
etched into a dream
that grips your shoulders
and the only way to release this tension
that rides on top of you
is to treat these songs as an instruction:

it was written like a manual.

Hip-Hop has everything to do with everything.

She doesn't need to be defended,
        doesn't need to explain herself,
        doesn't need your permission.

Hip-Hop walks with the
hypocrisies and benedictions
of every art form
in our existence.

You only notice her now:
how fresh her hips swing,
how zealous her disciples are,
how scared you get when she
uses those big words in conversation
and you beg her,

Please,
Please,
Talk to Me in a Way I Can Understand.

Then you turn up the radio
and feel safe.

this is not a love poem
i just happen to love you

my roommates always give me shit
about being in love with everyone
which i dont really mind i do love
a lot of people and i do fall in love easily
of course ive fallen for girls on the bus ride to school
and ive loved my teacher for giving me his favorite book
i knew i loved her when she wrapped me tight
because she was worried about me
i knew i loved him when i needed a drink
and he bought me three and i needed to talk
and he listened i fall in love with peoples
delicate and the way they joke with their friends
and the way they flip pages and the way their
faces crinkle because fuck it its fun to do a weird face
but i am so in love with you
it is my favorite love i have
this one i have with you
and only you

Phở Đặc Biệt

There are two Pho restaurants in Portland that I enjoy.
The first is in downtown and the other is on NE 82nd.

At 82nd the walls are sticky with generations of immigrants
carving a slice of home outside of home. The floors are oily

because you can't wash away the history of our people so easily.
The flowers are plastic and dusty, like Grandma's house.

I always see an uncle or an aunt when I'm there. Someone always
sees me, Dang's son or Ngoc's boy. I say *chào chị, chào anh.*

Then the Pho comes to your table. It's too much magic to be
bottled: you put that shit in a giant bowl. You let the broth

dance on your tongue and revive your soul with a goodness that
only a mom in the kitchen wearing her áo dài from across the

Pacific knows how to cook. Downtown, the floors are clean
and shiny. The furniture is slick and I never know anyone

there. There are no cousins at the counter talking shit and trading
swears as carefree as we did in the Marlboro smoke haze of

a tiny two-bedroom house: the only one we could afford. The walls
are too slippery and can't hold silk paintings like Chi Binh's

house, let alone how her parents came to America. None of the
servers are family. The plants are real and 20-something

college kids water them when I'm here. This doesn't look
real. It feels packaged. I feel like I'm in a picture frame. It's

not for us. It's for them. I order in English. Then the Pho comes
and it tastes like being sick at home watching *The Price is Right.*

It dances the same and I notice in the kitchen a drift of smoke
and Vietnamese piercing the indie selections like the twist of lime

swimming through the story of family; sitting in a giant bowl.

I see the smiling faces downtown as I do on 82nd. The magic

is in the food. It tastes so good. We don't dilute it. We know
how much it means. Our story can't be bottled. We lick it clean.

My Relationship with America
Is an American Horror Story

|||which is to say|||

I keep hoping for it to get better
and then remember that keeping the
dishes in the cabinet doesn't prevent them
from being a mosaic on the kitchen tile.
I've slept here my entire life and
all I see are ghosts.

|||which is to say|||

I'm not sure if this is a house or a home.
Does it matter how long I've stayed here?
What if it's haunted?
Are the angry spirits going to
drag me into the walls like
the other tenants
who lived here?

|||which is to say|||

How do I live? Some days
I know how to clean out the
monsters in the attic. Other nights
I retreat into my room and cringe
at every backward noise in the hall;
at every wrong sound in the closet.

|||which is to say|||

The only thing to do is slay the
thing that haunts. This ghoul of the past
that demands my blood and chews
on my children while my hands have
never fought anything.

|||which isn't to say|||

They can't.

i know i cant sing but i still will

today i am holy
and full and realized
to make up for the
loss of a thousand
yesterdays
i blessed my bedsheets
in sweat and turned my
body outside in only
for the world to see
aint shit changed
these altars
have not been altered
my love is sanctified
and it can forgive you
for loving me
there are nights
these arms turn wreckage
and the night sky
spings midnight
across my forehead
i fall into myself
as a reminder:
i am a split ocean

Dear Mark Wahlberg,

It has come to the attention of the public eye
that you are requesting a pardon for a crime you committed over
25 years ago. When you were 16, filled with intoxicants
a no-good Boston street punk, you assaulted
two Vietnamese men.

Some suggest you want this pardon only so you can obtain
a liquor license and expand your burger restaurant, Wahlburgers,
into California and across the nation. You said you want this
pardon because the weight bears too heavy on your body,
and come on bended knees, asking for forgiveness.

You know what I think, Mark?

I think,
you are just like me,
and understand that the perfect burger
must come with the perfect drink
and this is all for the love of burgers!
I completely get it.

If you're biting into one of your famous
BBQ Bacon Burgers topped with
white cheddar, bacon, avocado,
fresh jalapeños, and barbeque sauce,
it's not a complete meal unless
you have a frosty beer to go with it!

You're just like me!
You love burgers that much!

What would you recommend with it?
I think a clean, crisp pilsner would complement
the heaviness and salt of the white cheddar and bacon,

but what would you pick, Mark?

What skull would you crack open
What beer would you crack open
to enjoy the burger with?

And you know what,
let me ask you more about the patty.
You probably press them yourself!

With hands like yours
so acclimated to grinding flesh,
to render unconscious
to render the fat.

Because this pardon is just for the burgers, right?

Not because you struck Thanh Lam
with a 5-foot-long wooden plank
and left him mashed meat after spitting
Vietnam Fucking Shit. You were 16.
You were drunk, you were high
(high off the vision of these burgers, right?
drunk off the Thanksgiving Burger you would serve, right?).

You were trying to rob Lam for the beer
he was loading into his store.
You just wanted a perfect pairing
25 years in advance.

Not because later you found Johnny Trinh,
turned him pulverized muscle, and people
say you blinded him—it wasn't about that,
or the fact that he was a Slant-Eyed Gook.

You were caught up as a kid from the mean side
of your neighborhood; it was a different time;
things have changed; you have changed;
why does it matter who you were then
if you are who you are now!

Because you are just like me!
And they look just like me.

Erase the crimes that you committed
and you won't have to face them again.

Turn the blind eye
after all these years.

Say it was for your conscious.
Say it was for your soul.
Say it was for your burger empire
and you wanted to make more money.

The Daily Mail interviewed one of your victims, Mark.
They asked Johnny Trinh
about the assault, and he said,
Oh, He Was Just A Kid.
I Lost My Eye Before That In The War.
He Has My Forgiveness.

You have his blessing.
He doesn't even care.
He said he doesn't know who you are
and hasn't watched any of your movies!
He does not care!

Go on.
Get your pardon.
Clean your record.
Bite into your favorite burger
and taste blood.

On Trying to Explain to the Eye-Rolls in ENG 395 Why It Always Has to Be about Race

For starters, because it is about race. There's a topic that draws perfect pitch on your heartstrings—it tugs and twangs the chords perfectly—and you can't help but talk about it. You defend it nail, tooth, and hammer to the very end. For me, race isn't that topic. Burgers are. For me, race is not a topic. Race is a shadow painted permanently on my first bedroom walls—I never noticed how dark it was until I got older and my eyes focused and my chest illuminated. This is when the churning in my stomach began, too. Try to imagine it like an optical illusion: once you see it, you can't not see it. And so you keep witnessing this presence creep with tendrils; this car crash where you are the only person in both vehicles but you aren't driving; this rolling thick fog and you get yourself wrapped in it and your body shakes and you shiver but you never let your voice tremble. I hear your arguments, you Devil's advocate, which I appreciate, I really do. I see the dance shoes tied perfectly on your tongue and the way your contentions hold tension like the world's only dance floor: it's impressive. That takes hard-boiled work. But imagine never being able to take off that fancy attire. Picture your speech dressed for court every day. How tired your words must get, always being so stern and formal and infallible. An infinite fatigue. I would love to give it a rest. But I don't get to sleep it off. This thing wakes me up every time I start to dream. Nightmares are the only time it leaves me alone. So I don't sleep. I don't get to sleep. Even if I wanted to sleep. And believe me, I do. I'm exhausted.

On Riots

I don't know what you
expected would happen.

Drop a glass and it breaks.
Put fire to paper and it burns.
Fall and a stranger offers a hand.
Cause and effect.
Action and reaction.

Hands have been kept
in the air for so long
you forgot that they
can come down and
push back.

"The only motive
was motivation."

-Childish Gambino

5 p.m. in Bloomington

and we drive again we live out of these
suitcases and im feeling like our glamour
shines through car fatigue that we wear
tight on our skin im convinced im
dreaming weve been through a dozen states
and not one of them has been regret wasnt
i destined to a textbook-shaped coffin today
there was a test right but now now
these days are cup runneth over with
joy and blacktop like im living
lucky like im making the days that i will
fondly leaf through in three decades all
because we have a car and we have the
stories and we have the stage all because
we have the audacity to leap

Chance the Rapper Saves the World!

Chance the Rapper
loves the world so much.

He's got a smile so big
it's currently under consideration
to become a national monument.

His heart has arms that
keep us wedding warm.

Chance sings.
Like a lot.

Says it's the best way to get flowers
growing up strong and we need blossoms.
We need more gardens for more bouquets
since it's graduation season.

His laugh is sunset
pomp and circumstance and
every time we throw our hands up at his concerts
I swear there's another kid
who just tossed up his cap.

Drake says he's hardly home but always reppin'
but Chance is always home, always reppin',
always ready to give you a blanket and
hot chocolate because
it is so cold in his city.

If you spin around and say
South Side Chicago
three times,
Chance appears
with a pair of mittens
just for you.

His father, Ken Williams-Bennett,
used to be an aide to the mayor and
Obama. They worked real hard
on the Change Committee and now

Ken is a representative for the
US Department of Labor.

He always dreamed of getting his son
into the family business.

He succeeded!
Kind of.

Chance lives with change
and feels how powerful hope can be
in rainbow hands.

Decided to pursue it
in his own wonderfully everyday way.

Begins a movement to make his
home so strong that they
don't have to lift guns anymore.

He has seen loved ones
twist away in the wind
and has felt so heavy.

He hates fireworks because
they sound like bullet songs,
knows how hard it is to be
an alive boy on stage rapping with
the ghosts of all his friends
who he's older than now.

If you crack open Chance's heart,
a thousand cardinal skeletons will fly out,
and one fledgling
will puff his little loud chest,
with his too-big heart
and tweet
#faithinaction
#putthegunsdown
#savechicago

In September 2011
Chance's best friend, Rodney Kyles Jr.,
joined the flock of birds

inside Chance's heart.
Ken remembers how
it could have been
his son who died.

In May 2014,
Chance starts a campaign,
begging the boulevard air
to be muted of cannons.
Chance put a parade on his back
and Chicago went 42 hours
without a single shooting reported.

While the people are shouting
and angry and on fire,
all wanting to clench and clash,
Chance catches their hands
with Sunday Candy palms.
Pries open scarred knuckles
and kisses the inside as gentle
as you cradle water.

On July 30, 2014,
Chance becomes golden
and makes all of us kids again
by turning Lollapalooza and the world
back into magic by singing us a song
we all know the chorus to

And I say: Hey!/
What a wonderful kind of day/
Where we can learn to work and play/
And get along with each other/

so high school

after we first kissed
we joked about how it was so high school
the park bench the view the past-curfew
evening that draped around us
as we draped around each other
this group hug at a sleepover
when its gotten an hour too late
and youve gotten an hour too little of sleep
and you start talking about the big stuff

so high school
and we laughed and our teeth waltzed
in the tandem ballroom of our mouths
and we laughed and our tongues exchanged
pleasantries and corsages and we laughed
and we smiled and i didnt know then
but i know now that that first kiss
was the first and only push needed
to power our perpetual motion machine

this a lesson in eternity
this the taste of an eon
this so high school
because everyone thinks high school
lasts forever
and in regards to this
theyre right.

God Save the Selfie

My generation,
is the most selfish, entitled, and narcissistic
of all the generations ever.

Even if that were true,
so the fuck what?

We are the millennials
and the world can bow down to
all the dope shit that we do!

This is #nofilter
This is GPOY
This is every selfie Sunday,
transformation Tuesday,
and fuck you Friday that we've
been too busy to address.

Are we selfish because we are
demanding a spot for us in history?
We, too busy burning the candle
at every end due to our insatiable blaze for more.
This fire we cradle like Prometheus did—
a gift for the rest of mankind.

Funny how being selfish
looks so much like survival.
Looks like extracurriculars,
part-time jobs, and college graduations
planned like a perfect wedding.

Looks like the fish in the barrel shooting back,
Looks like loans that Atlas couldn't even shoulder,
Looks like all-nighters since we can't even afford sleep.

We are entitled.
We expected a home to move into and instead
got the house buckling in the floodwaters.

We are repairing every problem
left behind for us

including the kitchen sink.

We, fixers of the previous tenants
because the landlord doesn't do shit!

Of course we feel entitled.
Look at what your generation did before us!
Consider the fists of Mike Tyson knocking down giants.
We feel the rattle Nirvana crooned and
are warmed by your *Three's Company* home.

We learned from the best.
Why settle when you can grow cities
and monuments out of the old?
You taught us that.

Told us to connect with the world,
and now we do it faster at
120 megabits per second.

The selfie-obsessed generation—
What, like it's bad that
we want to remember our lives?

That even deep inside this
unrelenting precariousness of tomorrow
we will want to look back
on today,
on yesterday
and think,
Look At How Far We Have Gotten.

We are not narcissistic.
We just like looking at ourselves,
and our friends, and keeping up
with their everyday since we've made
every part of life extraordinary to capture.

So yes, we are going to Instagram that meal,
and yes, we are going to tweet that conversation.
The White House has a Twitter account!

We are all singing in this dubstep choir—
remixes exist because there are songs

that are so good they need to be played
again and again and again.

Are your college memories that much
different from ours? Caffeine never changes.

Are your late-night diner meals
better than late-night Taco Bell?
This is still a family meal.

Are you really going
to claim a higher severity
on your game of Monopoly
over our game of Smash Bros. Melee?

Both destroy friendships!
Nothing will be the same afterward.

The revolution has never been televised.
But you still found a way.

This time,
it's being told with our voice.
Sit down and listen.

Or at the very least,
watch us on BuzzFeed,
because we know you love that shit.

when asked where i would put the remains of my worst year

i said

put the ashes
in my mouth
in my food

lay it where I lay my head
line it in my t-shirts
and slip it under the
soles of my shoes

put the murderous
in my fingers as I
lace them
to pray
to write
to clean myself

turn everything charred
swallow the bloody
       blade
       first

keep the handle
keep the ways I held on
retire them to the toolshed

break only in case of emergency

i dont need these
right now
i dont think i will need them
ever again
i survived the fire
i have the killing to prove it
look at my skin
its iron forged

my oldest brother sits down to write a poem about our childhood

these are those golden days
basketball until the sun rusted
then run home

our feet raindrops
on the cracked sidewalk

open the kitchen door
with everything
smelling like
fish sauce

creep into the night
after Mom went to bed
and this is when we started sharing
the world with each other

we poured rainbows
in our dark hours
that tucked themselves
in our darker corners

we felt like gods
as we decorated immortality
through our spines

our fingertips twisted and lifted the seas
and we were legend
combed the ocean floor
for treasure
picked a garland of coral and seaweed
and placed it on my crush's doorstep

we are really out here now
us

fish gilled

boyish breathing
water kids
trading obscenities and contraband

while keeping a 4.0 close to our chest
and a 40 closer on our breath

look how golden it is
look how golden we are becoming

Kanye West Prays to Himself
after Clementine von Radics

praise the car crash that
could not   kill me
the windy jungle that
i am   king   of

thank you lord for
making me   in your image
for giving me your bravado

                              (who else has the arrogance
                              to create worlds simply
                              because they can?)

i use these hands
to gossamer
the sound waves
to story
the failure
turned   hallelujah

my brother's shadow/ remember how it eclipsed and i only
saw the halo of gold outlining his figure/ a flawless tracing

i am the gold tracing   now
i am the halo flawless now

and when the bullies from before pressed their
spit against me/ stuck to my skin like a sermon/
i washed off the poison with this holy sweat

            o holy
            o holy

speaking of my mother
this is the thesis of her soft body
hardening through work and blessing at home

            for the
            before it's too late
            for the

if i only had the chance
for the
for the's

i am now everything i needed
when i was a flower
being trampled

i am now earth and rain
            sun and air

i shelter
as hard as
i storm
now

The Miracle

Everyone I love has superpowers
and they will tell you that their origin story
did not make them who they are.

The people I look up to do not tell me that their
Uncle Ben,
destruction of Krypton,
night of the opera,
is what made them strong.

The people I look up to do not tell me that their
drug addiction,
alcoholism,
grief,
is what made them strong.

The ability to become
after the worst thing sledgehammers you
is what makes them great.

My mom does not tell me that her
story is what made her super.

I was born and bore witness to her
immense strength. So far as superheroes go,
she is the most overpowered.

With a frame of 4' 10"
Ngoc Tran redefines
comic book badassery.

Super Strength:
In one hand she has carried
four sons and tossed their sorry selves
through college and with the other
made my father, an unmovable mountain,
a pebble smoothed into the shape of her palm.

Intelligence:
Such gems like,
Do It Right Once Or Do It Wrong Three Times

Don't Be Sorry, Just Make Sure You Don't Do It Again
and the world's favorite:
Of Course I Know Everything. I'm Your Mom.

Telepathy:
All the times I thought
I was being sneaky as shit but
she was letting me
get away with it.

Clairvoyance:
She sees ghosts too! She still sees
her father like when she was seven,
still hanging in the kitchen after
he found out the communists were going
to take him away. Still drifting in her mind,
back and forth, a pendulum ticking
away her innocence.

She hears ghosts too
She hears the cries of my sister.
Still feels her small form, all bundle of light,
all star glow, gone as soon as she
shined in our world.

Resilience:
All she could do was watch.
Watch her mother's wedding ring
spirit away into the captain's pocket,
jingling with all the other boat people's
ticket out of the only home they had ever known.
Watch countries deny refugees of safety,
deny humanity, deny their existence.
Watch days crawl in a reeducation camp,
where she learned nothing but adversity.

Immortality:
She should have died.
Became a statistic about
Vietnamese immigrants
who never made it,
another prisoner of Viet Cong,
and a shouting point for
American protestors to

end a war
she called childhood.

And yet she stands.
Stands as a lesson to prove
how incredible we can be.

She has never let her
tragedy trump her triumph.

Never accepted that this
was all there was.

Never waited for a miracle
to grant the miracle I call Mom.

Only stitched my cape and told me

Fly!

The Engine

My dad got to this country
and saw all these
magnificent metal beasts
roam the streets:
each stronger and more glitter
than the last.

He told me,
America Loves Cars,
So, I Decided To Learn Everything About Them.
Someone Will Always Be Needed for Repairs.

We don't talk much, my dad and I.
Speak a total of 13 words when we drive home
and let the hum of the pavement fill in the rest.

My dad likes cars because
they're easier than people.
People don't have a check engine light,
            don't have a dashboard,
            don't tell you if something's wrong.

But cars,
      cars are   always honest.
    My dad is   always honest.

He doesn't talk much,
but lets his motor oil hands
speak for him.

Growing up, my brothers and I
never learned much about cars.
Four sons of a mechanic and not one
of us could replace a blown tire.
My dad never taught us.
Said he'd be around forever to fix our cars.
Plus, we'd be college men,
we'd be doing more important things
with our hands.

He never talks about love

but he always shows it.

So while my dad
teaches me to drive,
he tells me,
Listen To The Car.
Cars Tell You What's Wrong,
But Only If You Listen.

And I'm trying to listen,
listen to the whir of the engine,
pistons pumping fire and gasoline
as we cruise down Powell and
I think of the power to get
metal, father, and son
down the boulevard
and I hear my dad's heart.

I hear this heavy machinery,
all ignition and patience as I
forget to switch my blinker on,
go too fast in a school zone,
and my dad tells me to check my mirrors,
                    check my blind spots,
                    check my weaknesses,
                    tells me to listen.

My dad has been listening his entire life.
Never once flipped on the emergency brake,
kept sugar out of his gas tank,
turned the key and carried us with him.

His heart is getting weaker though.
Nothing lasts forever.
Some things you can only prevent
from breaking further.

I try to find the owner's manual to my father,
try to reassemble the engine of his childhood
and see what steered him here.

But his make is of another generation:
something I can't understand,
something I don't find instructions to,

something his dashboard refuses to show.

There is so much mileage on my father's bones,
spots in the road never ventured
because he never took us there.
Told us Dead End.
Told us Wrong Way.
Told us Turn Around.

I don't know what he is hiding in his workshop,
what corroded secrets he harbors
like rusted ghosts in a junkyard.
All I know is I want my hands
to look like they have been dipped in oil,
to look like they have done something important:
like a mechanic's,
like my dad's.

I want to be like my dad:
Who carries you out of
the backseat into your bed;
who lets you sit on his lap
and turn the wheel;
who always reminds you
to buckle your seatbelt.

Dad, I'm listening now.
I know you won't tell me
when something is wrong.

It's okay.
Let's just drive instead.
I'll listen,
I promise.

The Best American Poetry published michael derrick Hudson when he used the name of a girl he went to high school with, Yi-Fen Chou. He said it would help his chances of getting published.

michael derrick hudson
Changes His Name to Ngoc Tran

and my Mother's skin fits him like
a head on a wall,
trophy in a case,
history told by the victors.

michael tries out telling his new story
and the words avalanche out of his mouth,
every original now syllable white, cold, and
bland, but the belle of every dinner party
he attends. Tell Me More! his guests squeal
and without hesitation he talks about how
proud he is of Us. he raised four brown boys
all on the strength of his hands.

(which are too soft and pale
to have ever known the sweet
bloody labor of an immigrant)

Then drapes himself in the car business
Hiep Dang started from the ground up.

(he cuts out pieces of my Father's
tapestry to decorate his narrative
small detail easily fixed
whiteout edit an erasure)

he lets his tongue parade in broken English.
Exotic! they tell him.

(stupid, they tell Us)

he takes snapshots of Our American Dream
and they frame it and give him a gallery.
his picture: 1,000 words.

                                        (Our picture: 1 word = thief)

michael is such an innovator.
he writes such wonderful tales,
steals them out of thin air.

                                        (since We are no longer there
                                            no longer taking space
                                            no longer having names

That Was Just The Wind,

                                        he says at his poetry readings
                                    when We howl and gust and tornado)

but
his body is too weak
he cannot carry us like my Mother
Her skin gives him fever
something starts clawing out
from his insides gnashing
desperate to breathe to be born
Me and My Three Brothers
start crawling out of his throat
fistfuls of our Father
clutched in knuckles
We smooth the Familial Cloth
stuff his arrogant mouth with it
make michael choke on our pronunciation
he told Our story
one too many times and his colony
could not hold Us any longer
We broke free and We took back
the Names the Recipes
the Home the Country
the Air by god We took
back Our Air and We filled it with
our Good Good Brown Bodies
too hot to touch
We melt his trophies
smolder the wall
burn his house down

but We leave his name alone

70

his books remain untouched
instead
We cross out his pseudonym
and underneath it
We write
michael derrick hudson

We will not borrow from him
We will create in spite of him

are

you

proud

of

me?

Acknowledgements

Cue the music: I will be going over time.

We have a romantic notion about the artist trapped alone in their room creating genius all by themselves. That never happens. The greatest work comes through a community. Through love, family, friends-this is where the art comes from.

Thank you to my Mom and Dad for being the only parents I could ever want. You both have taught me where I am from and where I can go and the only thing that determines this is myself. Thank you to Richard, Eric, and John for being my first friends and role models and for teaching me all the things older brothers need to teach their baby bro.

Thank you to my two longest friends, Andres and Jake. I've known you two for over two thirds of my life and here's to making that fraction get closer to one. For my 7th and 8th grade basketball team and coach for letting me know that it doesn't matter how you get back up. For Ms. Evans, I will never forget how much you believed in me. For Ms. Mac for being wonderful every morning of Advisory and for coining the ! in my name.

Thank you to Cleveland High School weirdly enough for introducing to me to so many of the influences who I hold in my heart always. To Whitney, you were always there to listen to me. To Mr. Graham, thank you for letting me write raps in lieu of essays. To Jane, because of course I need to thank my Drama teacher. To Ms. Adana who showed me every day how caring is a super power. To my Leadership class of '11 and '12 for letting me cry. To Improv Club for letting me laugh. And of course, Mr. Gonzales, for being my Speech and Debate Coach, Senior English teacher, and hand on the wheel when I needed guidance.

Thank you to Reed and Griffin for every late night where the only goal was to make something. To Anna Connor for listening to a lot of first draft poems when I still wasn't sure if I was going to be a poet. Thank you to Eric for redefining the word loyalty. For Sara Pearlman for always answering my texts and sending me love.

Thank you infinitely to the Portland Poetry Slam. Without you, a 17 year-old Bieber-haired kid would have never been able to tell his stories. To everybody who watches, reads, and pours their spirit into the slam, thank you so much. Thank you to the Portland Poetry Slam in its many forms. Thank you to Robyn Bateman who has time and time again shown me how to be a leader, a writer, and a good person. Stephen Meads, thank you for challenging me ever since I got to the slam to work harder. For my team members, since I would never have been able to write this without you all. Eirean Bradley, you taught me how to scream. Davey Mac, you taught me how to trust in myself. Brenna Twohy, you taught me how to find strength in vulnerability. Doc Luben, you taught me how to be honest. Leyna Rynearson, you taught me how to be fierce and uncompromising. Erin Schick, you taught me how to be solid and to have resolve. Finn Greenseth, you taught me how to throw your heart into the open.

Thank you to my dorm mates in Henderson Hall who would stay up with me in the lounge to listen to my first drafts after I was sure I wanted to be a poet. Thank you to Lilly Solano for the wonderful art and warmth. To Alejandro and Alexi for being my first readers and for being great friends. To Joss and the late night drives and Hamilton. Thank you to Val for having someone to side eye with in class. Amanda, thank you for being in my corner. To the Rattle Boys, I mean, let's be real, you guys are the squad.

To my CUPSI team, Hannah, Dante, Maxine, and Annalee: thank you for believing in my softness and thank you for being the easiest team to coach. And for being the best people to drive at 3AM towards the airport with.

To Paul Peppis and Corbett Upton, you two are the kind of professor and person I want to be.

Thank you to everyone at Where Are You Press for giving me a place to put my poetry. Thank you to Lora Mathis for the incredible cover art and all the sweetness. Thank you to Elizabeth von Radics for editing the book and for every good luck text before a slam.

Thank you to Novella Café for putting up with my terrible work schedule and for covering for me when I needed to go do poems somewhere. And for letting me read and write on the job and for the caffeine.

Thank you to everyone who has shown me love. I could not have done this without you.

Thank you to Clementine, my better half, my love, and for always making me want to be a better person every day.

Previously Appeared In

"On Riots" was previously published in The Rising Phoenix Review under the name "Baltimore."

"in which the poet apologizes again" was previously published in Voicemail Poems.

"The Swallowed" was previously published in The Harpoon Review and Autumn Sky Poetry Daily.

Also from Where Are You Press

This Is How We Find Each Other
Fortesa Latifi

Sullen Girl
Kiki Nicole

Give Me A God I Can Relate To
Blythe Baird

Forgive Me My Salt
Brenna Twohy

Healing Old Wounds With New Stitches
Meggie Royer

Dream Girl
Clementine von Radics

The Women Widowed To Themselves
Lora Mathis

It Looked A Lot Like Love
Kristina Haynes

Until I Learned What It Meant
Yena Sharma Purmasir

Where Are You Press was founded in 2013. We publish beautiful books of inspired, honest poetry by women, people of color, and other marginalized voices. We are based in Portland, Oregon.